Outdoor Secrets

by
Margaret P. Boyle

Illustrated by
Augusta T. Tappan

Outdoor Secrets
ISBN: 978-1-61634-059-9

Originally published in 1903
By A. Flanagan Company
Chicago

This edition edited by Sonya Shafer
© 2009, Simply Charlotte Mason, LLC
All rights reserved.

Published and printed by
Simply Charlotte Mason, LLC
P. O. Box 892
Grayson, Georgia 30017
U. S. A.

Cover Design: John Shafer
Cover Art: Original frontispiece
Production Date: August 15, 2012

www.SimplyCharlotteMason.com

*And Nature, the old nurse, took
 The child upon her knee,
Saying "Here is a story book
 Thy Father has written thee."
 —H. W. Longfellow*

Outdoor Secrets
by Margaret P. Boyle

What Is Within

How the Apple Blossom Came Back 9
The Century-Plant's Wish 13
The Uninvited Guest 17
What the Golden-Rod Did 23
The Horse Chestnut's Name 27
A Rainy Day Sermon 33
The Selfish Salvia 37
Who Knocked? 41
A Disobedient Tree 47
The Bumblebee's Mistake 53
A Brave Plant 59
The Sower .65
The Baby Plants' Bed Coverings 71
A Family Quarrel 77
Two True Stories about Robins 83
The Idle Chipmunk 89
The Troubled Apple-Tree 93

Outdoor Secrets

How The Apple Blossom Came back

Once upon a time, not so very long ago, there stood in a large orchard a beautiful Apple-Tree. All through the long winter it had held out bare branches. The March sun whispered to it that spring had come. But the cold March winds were not a bit polite, and would say: "No, it hasn't."

At last, however, Apple-Tree began to feel so warm and comfortable that she thought the March sun was right, and began to think of getting a spring gown. The warm April rains helped her, and her buds opened and grew, first into tiny leaves and then into larger ones, until Apple-Tree was wearing a beautiful apple-green dress. All through April she wore it and was very happy. Then, as the trees about her put on bright colors, and she saw Peach-Tree in pink and Cherry-Tree and Pear-Tree in white, something seemed to tell her to try what she could do.

I am sure she could never have succeeded without help,

How the Apple Blossom Came Back

but with the showers, the gentle winds, and the warm sun as dressmakers, Apple-Tree's green dress was soon covered with lovely pink and white flowers. And the air all around seemed as sweet as though she carried many handkerchiefs with different perfumes on each. Then Apple-Tree felt very glad and proud and was much pleased when every one who passed said: "Oh, see, how lovely!"

But only a week or two later a damp wind and cold rain came and beat down on her spring suit until it was quite spoiled. Then Apple-Tree was so sorry that she let her teardrops fall with the rain. Kind Mother Nature did not scold her at all, but only said: "Don't cry about the blossoms, dear; sometime you will see them again."

So all summer long Apple-Tree looked and waited, for she knew that Mother Nature always told the truth. Her arms grew full of apples, and sometimes they seemed too heavy to hold any longer. Whenever she was very tired, there would come the whisper: "Wait a little longer. Your time is coming—the time when you will find the blossoms."

And at last, one sunny September day, one yellow apple after another slipped from her hold and lay on the grass beneath. While Apple-Tree was wondering what would happen, a lady and her little boy wandered through the orchard and stopped to pick and eat some apples.

"Robert," said the mother, "have you ever seen the blossom in an apple?"

"Oh, no, mother; please show it to me!"

Apple-Tree bent her tall head so that she might hear and see. Could it be that now she was to find the flowers she had lost in the spring?

The lady carefully cut an apple all around, half-way

between the blossom end and the stem. And as she laid the halves before her little boy, she pointed to the blossom which showed plainly in both pieces of the apple. And Apple-Tree held the rest of her fruit tightly in her arms, sure that in each one was a blossom she had loved months before.

The Century Plant's Wish

Years before Apple-Tree had found her blossom, at the time when Robert's mother came as a bride to her new home, she brought with her, among other things, a tiny Century-Plant. All there was of it were two or three stiff little leaves. But it was placed in a beautiful conservatory with the stately palms, the graceful ferns, and all the rare and lovely plants that lived there.

As the years passed on, the leaves grew a little longer and a little broader, and one or two more were added, but that was all. So, even in that beautiful home, life for the Century-Plant was very dull. The years were just the same: all winter long she was shut up in the hot-house, and when the days and nights had grown warmer, showing that summer had really come, she was placed in some conspicuous place on the lawn. The only real change she ever knew was an occasional transplanting into a larger box.

So the Century-Plant began to murmur, and to wish, oh, so many things! Why could she never be set in the ground like some of her winter companions, the brilliant Jacqueminot, or American Beauty Roses, the Lilies, the Carnation Pinks, or even the sweet little Violet? She knew that when she was out of doors she had the same warm sunshine, and the same refreshing rain as these friends of hers had, but that did not satisfy her. She wanted to live in the earth and send her roots out into it, as plants were intended to do.

But she could have borne this trouble if only she might have had some flowers to show, or could once have been admired for her loveliness. The Rose family, all the Pinks, the Heliotrope—in fact, many of the plants about her— would often get sweet new gowns. And visitors to the conservatory would admire them, or sniff their fragrance, saying: "Oh, how lovely!" or, "Isn't it perfectly beautiful?"

Even the Palms and the Ferns, though they never showed a blossom, were praised for their lovely greens.

But when visitors reached her corner they would say only: "Oh, this is a Century-Plant. Curious thing, isn't it? Has it ever bloomed?"

And always would come the same answer: "No, not yet."

It was hard always to be called "curious," like some strange wild animal.

The fair young bride who had brought the tiny plant to her home grew gray and wrinkled. One day she failed to visit the flowers; the gardener said she was ill, and the Century-Plant saw her no more. Robert and the other children who had played about the Century-Plant on the lawn grew into men and women, and their little ones toddled about the box that held the old plant, and still there were no flowers.

Even though Century-Plant had grown very tall by this time, she still had to keep on wishing that she had something to wear besides the same old green and white.

The Century-Plant's Wish

For many years Mother Nature had promised her something else, and it had never come yet. So sometimes she almost gave up hope.

But there came a day, when, in answer to her wistful sigh, she was told: "Just be patient; you haven't much longer to wait."

And Century-Plant really began to think so herself. A day or two later a strange thing happened.

The gardener was bending over her when he exclaimed: "Bless my stars, there's a bud! I must go tell the ladies."

Then Century-Plant knew that at last her wish was to be realized, and the thought of having a flower of her own made her glad and happy, notwithstanding her old age.

Gentle whispers went through the hot-house. The Violet sweetly breathed: "I am so glad Century-Plant is going to have some blossoms."

And the Rose answered: "So am I."

As for Century-Plant herself, she felt quite above her neighbors now, for the wonderful new flower stalk kept getting taller and taller, until from its top she could look down even on the stately palms. And still she grew, until her tall head touched the roof. Now, after all these years, must she stop for lack of room? Century-Plant trembled through all her leaves at the thought; but the thoughtful gardener had provided for this, too, and the roof was lifted higher and higher until the stalk was thirty or forty feet in the air. Then Century-Plant was so full of pride that she hardly noticed the perfume Violet was sending up to her.

At last the curious flowers up at the top of the stalk opened and looked so strange that it seemed as though Century-Plant were wearing an imported bonnet. People came from far and near to gaze at her.

And though they used to exclaim, it was much in the way they always had, and the remarks were generally: "How queer! Have you ever seen one before?"

And it seemed as though they still loved the sweet modest flowers best. Century-Plant never noticed that, but was very happy so long as her new bonnet kept fresh and bright. But one day the flowers fell one by one, and the stalk began to grow so limp that at last that, too, dropped. Then Century-Plant, herself, began to feel very ill. Nothing she ate or drank seemed to agree with her. She had gained her wish, but was more unhappy than ever. Probably she never had known that when a Century-Plant has bloomed it must die. Day after day she faded away until one morning the gardener pulled the old plant up by the roots and threw it out on a brush heap.

Century-Plant's corner is empty now, and a banana palm takes her place on the lawn, but whenever some impatient young thing wishes that Mother Nature would hurry her plans a little, some wise old resident of the conservatory is sure to say: "Remember the sad end of poor Century-Plant."

The Uninvited Guest

The long, beautiful summer was nearly at an end. So some of the little people who live out of doors thought they would have a farewell party. It was not probable that they would ever meet again; for some of them life would end with this season. And most of the others would sleep through the long winter, and who knew what might happen during the six months' nap? They chose what they thought just the nicest place in the wide world for holding a party. As the day proved a beautiful one, everyone who had been invited came—which does not always happen when real folks have parties.

Among the guests were the Butterfly, in her satin gown of black and orange; the Cicada, prepared to help with the music; the Katydids, who really are not very pleasant visitors, because they contradict so much; the Beetles, fat, lazy and black, like most beetles; the Grasshoppers, who also are musicians, and had their wings in fine order; the Bees, who had gathered enough honey to last all winter; the Tree-Frog, and ever so many others.

They all had a merry time out on the meadow, and yet they were a little sad, too, for they knew that Jack Frost was coming soon, and that he would put an end to all their good times.

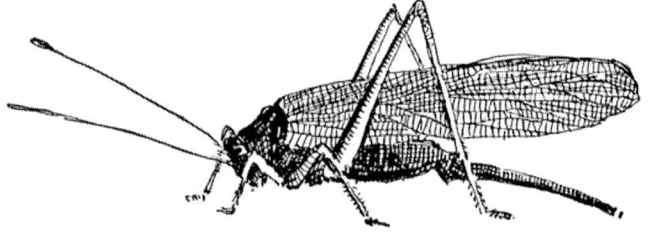

Just as they were the very jolliest, a strange thing happened. That was the arrival of a long, brown, wriggling Earth-Worm. Fortunately for the Earth-Worm, he has no eyes. So he could not see how cross all the little meadow people looked because he had come. I wonder if we should sometimes look cross just as they did, if no one had eyes to see us.

They did not invite him to stay, nor offer him any refreshments. Though, really, I think he would not have taken anything if it had been offered, for earth-worms do not care much for honey and the other things that this company were eating.

When they found that he did not notice their cross looks, they began to whisper to one another.

"Oh, dear!" said the Butterfly, "see that horrid, crawling Earth-Worm. I do dislike anything that crawls!"

"Yes," chirped the Cicada. "And only fancy, he lives in

the ground. How dreary that must be!"

"For my part I don't see how anyone can stand it," said the Beetle.

"Katy did," broke in a shrill voice.

"Katy didn't," said another.

"Yes, and they actually live after they are cut in halves," said the Tree-Frog. "I once knew an Earth-worm that met with such an accident, and then there were two of him, for the head part grew a tail, and the tail piece grew a head."

They did not mean the Earth-Worm to hear their unkind remarks. But he did hear, and they were very much surprised when he began to speak: "I am sorry I came to your party if you didn't want me, but I thought I'd like to come out once more before the cold weather gets here. And, really, you shouldn't feel so bad to see me crawling, for it is not so long ago that some of you used to crawl. Don't you remember, Miss Butterfly?"

The Butterfly thought with all her butterfly brain, and did recall a time, not so very long before, when she was a fat, crawling caterpillar. But she had a kind heart, if she was a little silly sometimes, so she said, "I'm sorry; I had forgotten all about my caterpillar days."

The Earth-Worm answered: "Very well, I'll forgive you. And as for living in the earth, I am quite contented there, for I have plenty to do. I really am not lonely, either, for I have a good many neighbors. One of you lived near me—or, rather, near my family—for seventeen years!"

At this, everybody looked at the Cicada, for there was an old story that everyone knew, about how it took the Cicada seventeen years to appear.

As for him, he was so ashamed that he wanted to change the subject at once, so he said: "Well, friend Earth-Worm, you said you were very busy. What do you do all the time?"

"Oh, I have to get the soil in good order—that is, make

it fine and soft so the tiny rootlets of all the green growing things can spread through it and thus give you something to eat. Were it not for us, many of you might go hungry. For if they could not send forth their roots, the plants could not grow. There would be no tender green leaves for Mr. Beetle, and certainly no flowers, and then where would Busy Bee go for his honey?"

"How do you know all that?" asked a Grasshopper. "I thought—"

"Katy did," interrupted some one.

"Katy didn't," said his sister.

At that they all laughed.

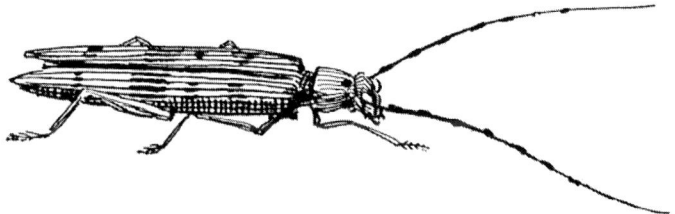

Then the Earth-Worm went on: "We Earth-Worms keep taking soil into our stomachs. We digest all of it that we can. In our stomachs is some kind of acid that acts on the rest of the soil and makes it fine and soft. After a while, we let this earth out of our stomachs and take in a fresh supply, until the soil all around us is so light and fine that the plants can grow fast and send out the tender green leaves many of you like to eat. But I must go now," and the Earth Worm began to wriggle away.

He couldn't go far, however, for one after the other had something nice to say to him. They told him he seemed to do more good in the world than any of them. They thanked him for all his hard work, too, which had really been so much help to them, though they had not known it. And all their kind speeches made the Earth-Worm feel very happy.

This was not their farewell party, after all. Before they separated they decided to hold one the next day. And you may be quite sure that they did not forget Earth-Worm then. Indeed, he was the first one to have an invitation, even before Katy-Did.

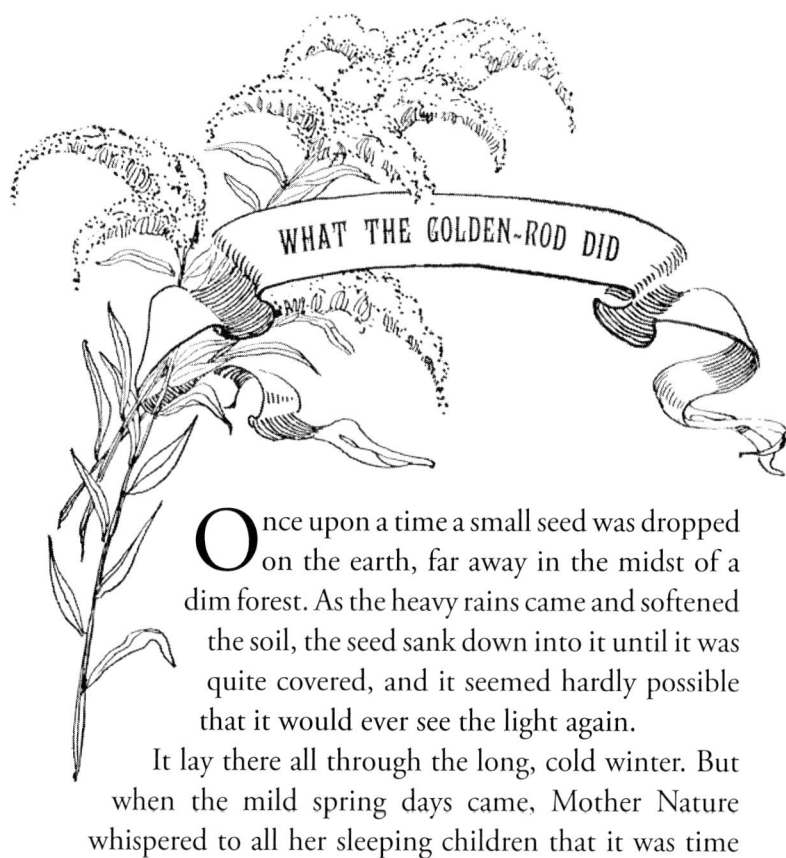

WHAT THE GOLDEN-ROD DID

Once upon a time a small seed was dropped on the earth, far away in the midst of a dim forest. As the heavy rains came and softened the soil, the seed sank down into it until it was quite covered, and it seemed hardly possible that it would ever see the light again.

It lay there all through the long, cold winter. But when the mild spring days came, Mother Nature whispered to all her sleeping children that it was time to be astir.

The little seed heard the whisper, and tried so hard to obey that it burst its hard shell in the effort, and sent a tiny shoot up toward the light. Mother Nature had known that was just what would happen, so she had softened the hard earth to let the green blade through.

Soon there were small green leaves, and then, in a little while, a nice growing plant. The sun smiled on it, and the rain wept over it, and at last a small lady in green appeared

between the green leaves. Taller and taller she grew, and day by day her green gown began to take on a yellow tint. The long sunny days grew cooler and shorter; the grasses and flowers that had lived all about the little lady in green began to fade and die. Even the trees that had sheltered her all her life began to act as though their work were done for a while and to let go their hold on their leaves. But the lady in green only grew more beautiful. Her gown changed into a lovely shade of yellow, and she became a beautiful feathery branch of golden-rod.

Still—strange though it may seem—the Golden-Rod was not really happy. Though she had not seen nearly every kind of flower, she knew what was done through all the floral kingdom. She had heard how the shy little Violets were so loved for their fragrance that friends sent them to one another as gifts, to be treasured carefully in costly vases, or perhaps to be worn lovingly by the receiver.

She had been told of the fame of the Roses, and that they were so sweet and beautiful that brides were glad to carry them, and they were welcome decorations in the most elegant homes. There were the Carnations, too, that brought cheer to sick-rooms, and made all who knew them glad with their spicy fragrance.

At last she could bear it no longer, and cried to Mother Nature to ask her if she must always be a lonely spray of golden-rod—if there were nothing she could do. Even the common Field Daisies and Clovers were often gathered and sent away to cheer poor little city waifs. But away in that dark forest no one could see her; not even a wild bee came to gather her honey.

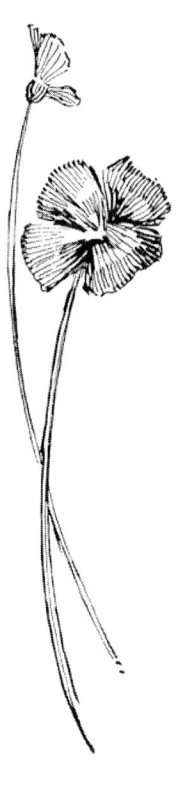

Mother Nature smiled as she heard the sorrowful cry. Then she answered, much as she had done to other children who had complained: "Wait a little longer, dear, and you will find your work. Everything in this whole round world has some work to do. Just be brave and patient, and yours will come to you."

The Golden-Rod knew that, like all good mothers, Mother Nature always tells the truth. So—though it was hard work, because it seemed to her that the cold days were coming fast—she tried to wait patiently and to hope.

One day a strange sound was heard—a very different sound from the twittering song of the birds, or the voices of the wild animals, or the sighing of the leaves. For the first time in Golden-Rod's short life a human voice was speaking near her. A hunter had followed a deer, far from the paths he knew, quite into the heart of the forest. And now, try as he would, he could not find the way out. Night was near; what was the poor hunter to do?

"If I could but find a bit of golden-rod," he said, aloud, "I should be all right, but I can't see even a single spray."

Little Golden-Rod waved her feathery head, with all her might, but she was so short that perhaps he would not see her; if only she could make a noise! But at last the hunter looked that way.

"Ah, here it is, thank God, pointing straight toward the north, as the golden-rod always does! I know the right direction now."

Then Golden-Rod hung her feathery head; Mother Nature's promise had come true. She had found her work, and a greater one than any of the flowers she had envied, for she had saved a human life.

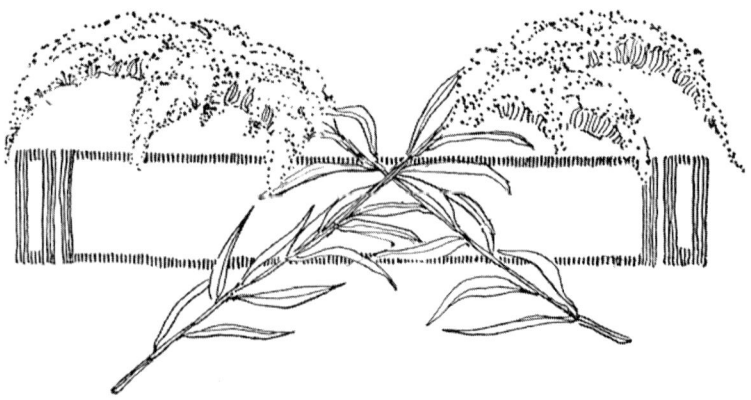

The Horse Chestnut's Name

There was a great commotion out on the lawn, and such a roaring among the trees that it seemed as though they were all trying to talk at once. The great Oak tossed its twisted branches with every fresh gust of wind. It was many years since that Oak had sprung from a tiny acorn, so it was quite the oldest inhabitant of the lawn. Perhaps it was for that reason that it was allowed to speak first and to tell its history.

"We Oak-Trees are very old. More than one of us has had a place in history. In England beautiful homes are built among us. Our wood is carved for ornament, and for handsome pieces of furniture. Ships are built of us and go sailing across the deep sea. We stand firmly in our places year after year, and each season drop tiny acorns on the ground. The rains beat upon these, they sink down into the earth, the little seed baby that is hidden in each one pushes its head upward and its tiny rootlets down, grows with all its might year after year, and at last is a big tree like me."

Very near the Oak was a stately Pine, which waved its feathery branches, sighed through every limb, and now bent its tall head as though to speak. "There is much for a Pine to tell. The Pines, too, are very old. Hundreds and hundreds of years ago, in the days of King Solomon, fir-trees and cedar-trees, which are close relatives of the pines, were used for building. If oak-trees are used for making the ships, pines make the masts which hold the big sails. And if oak-trees help in house-building, the pines and cedars do their part, too. And while the oaken furniture is for the rich, the pine makes cheaper kinds that the poor may use.

"Up in the cold Northland, the outside bark makes whole roofs of houses. The inner bark is twisted into ropes, or else it is pounded fine and made into bread. How do you think you would like pine-bread? It may do very well in countries where it is so cold that nothing else will grow, but I think most boys and girls would like wheat-bread better.

"But, really, we Pine-Trees are wonderful. For in Germany and Sweden the people soak the needles and then have them woven into blankets. But I rather think we are liked best by the little children when we are set up in the house on Christmas Day.

"It takes the pine seed-babies a long time to grow. In the spring there comes a queer greenish sort of flower. Then—not in the next autumn as with other fruits, but in a year from that—these flowers change into cones. The cones hang fast until the next spring and then fall to the ground with their seeds. The seeds seem to have hard work to grow, so many get lost. But there are some which fall into the earth, and at last make a tall tree, just as I have done."

There were more than one Maple on the lawn, and they would not be kept waiting any longer. They told that they bore every spring thousands of seed pods. At the bottom of every one was a green seed something like a pea. These fell thick and fast on the ground and in a little while sent up so many small trees that the gardener could not let them all live, but had to pull up many a one.

Like the Oak and the Pine, the Maple could tell of many a pretty bit of furniture which it could make. And there was one other claim which not another tree on that lawn could make—there was a special kind of Maple which gave out sap that formed luscious maple sugar. So they thought they, as well as the Pine-Trees, were the children's friends.

At that there came a sound from the Linden. It was a beautiful tree. Its branches had spread in every direction till it covered more space than the old Oak.

"It seems to me the children should love me," it said. "See what a fine shade I make for them to play in. Then the sweet flowers that come on my boughs every year are filled with honey, some of which I give up to every bee that comes. The bees store it away for themselves. But the children get some of it, and who ever yet heard of a boy or girl who did not like bread and honey?

"Bordering an avenue in Berlin, a city of Germany, there is so beautiful a row of us that the avenue is called 'Under the Lindens.' "

But before the Linden could tell any more about itself and its family, a Horse Chestnut, who had been very impatient for a long time, began: "Whatever the rest of you may tell, not one of you can tell how it got its name. But I can show everyone who cares to look.

"Two or three hundred years ago—in the sixteenth century, to be accurate—we were brought from Constantinople. There the people used to grind up our nuts for medicine, or for food for horses. So that, it is said, is the reason we were called Horse Chestnuts.

"But some of us think we know a much better reason. If this gale that I feel coming will only help me, I shall be glad to show you what it is. If you will look, you may find, all along my slender twigs, ridges and marks. Take a penknife and cut around one of these ridges. You will then see that it is just the shape of a horse's foot. Within is the dark spot like the frog in a real foot, and the little dots are the same in number as the nails in a horseshoe. Above is the bend like the knee of a horse, and to me that seems a good reason for being called a Horse Chestnut.

"There is another way in which I differ from other trees. Over each of my buds I have a thick coat. This is stuck together with something so sticky that through all the hard storms not a bit of rain or snow can reach the tiny leaves and blossoms that are hidden away inside. The busy bee that you may have often heard of takes this sticky substance, too, and puts it in the cracks of his hives to keep them warm and tight."

Just then a great gust of wind, probably the gale that Horse Chestnut had felt coming, blew a small Horse Chestnut bough right across our path. We were so busy looking along the bark for the horse's hoof—and finding it, too—that we never heard what the other trees had to tell.

A RAINY DAY SERMON

It was a very stormy Sunday morning—just the sort of morning when you would not expect many people to go to church, but to stay comfortably inside, watching the raindrops chase one another down the pane, or tumble as fast as they could into the nearest mud puddle. I suppose on such mornings the clergymen themselves think: "Dear me, I shall have to talk to many empty pews to-day; it won't matter so very much about my sermon." And they look and feel very solemn in consequence.

But this little minister of whom I am going to tell you looked just as cheery and bright as though the sun had been shining. In fact, he was so very unlike most reverend gentlemen that I must tell you about him. In the first place, he dressed very differently. Instead of a long black coat or a white surplice, he wore a coat of shaded brown, and just the prettiest red waistcoat, and on his feet were something you and I have never yet seen in the pulpit—bright brown shoes.

But though people admired his dress, his bright black

eyes and sweet voice charmed them more. You may have heard that it is a great thing for a public speaker to have a pleasant voice, so perhaps that is the reason this friend of ours never failed to please. If you could have seen his simple home you might have wondered that he could be so happy, for it was just made of mud with a straw or perhaps a hair bed inside. But that he had not a care in the world you need only look at him to see. So it appears that a beautiful home is not necessary to make one happy.

Years ago it was the custom to have the pulpit much higher than the pews, and after the preacher had climbed almost as many steps as though he were going upstairs, he could stand there and look down on his hearers. But of all the high, old-fashioned pulpits that ever were made, there never was one quite so far above the pews as this. Over the little minister was a beautiful canopy, and all about him were lovely green hangings. And he never even tried to look down on his hearers, or to wonder whether they would like what he had to say. Instead he was there just to deliver the message contained in his notes.

The choir were not all present that morning. Probably some of them thought it really was not worth while to sing in the rain. So, as there was no opening anthem, the congregation did not know when the sermon was about to begin, and were much surprised to hear the first clear notes.

There were persons of all ages represented in the audience, even to the baby—a mistake to take a baby to church in the rain, you say; this one was not in a pew, but lay in his crib moaning and fretting over the troubles, troubles, troubles, that make up so large a part of babyhood, and that grown-ups so often misunderstand. He was too young to know just what the preacher was saying, but it had a cheery sound as it came into his nursery, and so he stopped his troubled cry.

Two children, tired of their books and of the stay indoors which the rain enforced, began finding fault with each other, then disputing. Their voices grew louder and crosser, and soon, I am much afraid, there would have been a quarrel if just then they had not heard this part of the sermon: "Cheer up! Cheer up! Be good children!" They stopped to listen, then to wonder what it was, and by that time their quarrel was forgotten; they had grown cheerful, and once more were good children.

Another of the hearers was a woman, young and fair, and who once had thought all of life beautiful. But a great sorrow had come to her, and now, almost broken-hearted, she lay there, wondering if there were any good in life, and wishing, wishing that hers might end. Why should she try to be brave? Her skies looked as gray as those out of doors and her tears fell as fast as the rain.

She was too sad and troubled even to notice that there was preaching going on, until notes so loud were used to emphasize a point that even she heard and heeded. "Cheer up!" How could she, when there was so little left in life for her? But still, in spite of the rain, the glad, happy notes sounded, and unconsciously the broken-hearted listener absorbed their comfort. Her grief was too great to be healed, but for the sake of those about her, she would try to take up her life once more, and, hiding her heartache with a smile, live it out to the end.

There were others among the audience that morning

who needed help and comfort; somehow one never has to look very long in this big world for that kind of people.

In one corner, in his rocking-chair, sat an old man whose journey was almost done; many of his friends had gone on before, and now, lonely, feeble, and broken in health, he looked back with a sigh over his closing life. But, dull of hearing though he was, the gospel of good cheer came to his ears, also, and brightened and helped him. It told him that the friends he had lost were waiting for him in the land where one never grows old, and that he would soon meet them there; so he in his turn tried to cheer up.

And now, since so many of that morning's congregation went away comforted, surely it was no mistake to speak of him as a preacher, though he was only a robin singing in the rain.

The Selfish Salvia

Last summer there were two sisters living side by side. Their home was in a beautiful garden where rose bushes lifted their beautiful flowers, where mignonette made all the air sweet, where petunias tumbled about, trying to see which could grow the fastest, and where it was so lovely altogether that they surely should have been very happy.

They each had a beautiful bright scarlet gown, and looked so much alike that you and I could never have told the difference between them, except that one was a little taller than the other. But, though they looked alike, they were as different as could be, which we all know is often the case with sisters.

When I tell you that their name was Salvia, I am sure you will guess that they were flowers which grew and bloomed. Each of these flowers had hidden away—far out of sight, as people often keep their treasures—a tiny drop of honey.

One day that "Little Busy Bee" you may have heard of, saw their bright colors and flew straight toward them.

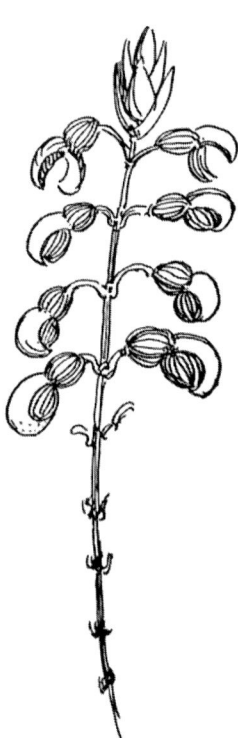

The younger saw him coming and said: "There comes one of those horrid Honey-Bees. I am not going to give him any of my honey, if he does want it."

But the other sister answered: "Why not, dear? They say that if we help the Honey-Bee, he in his turn will help us, and really we could easily spare him a little honey."

"Well, you can give him some if you want to, I don't expect to," answered the other Salvia, who was really rather fond of having her own way.

And just then, as the Honey-Bee came near, she held herself very straight on her stem, with her petals just as nearly closed as they could be. The Bee seeing this, paused only a second and then passed on to the older sister.

She was willing to give up her honey just as she had said she would be, and drew up her head and let her broad lip drop. In Mr. Bee stuck his head to get the honey. Then Miss Salvia was as polite as could be, and bent back her anther so that the little dust bag she carried with its load of pollen came plump down on the bee, covering all his back with the yellow powder called pollen. But the Bee did not seem to mind in the least. He sucked up all the honey he could, and then flew on to some other flower.

"There," said the younger, "what a goose you are! You have given away every drop of honey you had, and I have all of mine yet. Here comes another bee; he shan't have any, either, and you have none to give him. I think he will soon find he will have to go to some other part of the garden."

"Perhaps he will give us something," said number one.

"Nonsense! Whatever would a bee have to give a flower?" replied the other scornfully.

So when the Bee came it was much as it had been before: the elder was just as ready as she had been before, and this time even bent down her stigma. The Bee had been to another flower, so his back was all covered with pollen, that had been dropped on him from the little dust bag. And when the stigma—that is the little place where the flower keeps her seeds—bent over, it got covered with dust. But the younger blossom was just as tightly closed as she had been before, and the Bee passed her by.

Soon both the flowers began to fade and to drop their seeds, one by one, into the earth beneath.

Time passed and the seeds that fell from the generous

The Selfish Salvia

Salvia, which had been so ready to give her honey to the Bee, sent up strong green shoots. The seeds of the other failed to show a single sprout.

A great questioning went around the garden. And one plant after another asked why flowers that had grown side by side in the same ground, that had been warmed by the same sun, and been drinking in the same rain, should not have seeds alike.

Only Mother Nature could answer this question, and she said: "It is because one flower was generous, and the other selfish. When the Salvia opened her flower to give the Bee honey, he in his turn gave her all he had to give."

"What was that?" asked a young Aster.

"Pollen," said Mother Nature; "the yellow dust he had gathered from some other Salvia. It rubbed off on the stigma, then went down the tiny tube and helped the seeds to be strong, so that when their turn came they could grow. The selfish Salvia would not let the Bee have honey, so the Bee could not give her pollen. Consequently she had nothing to feed her seeds, and they were too weak to grow. My children, remember always that if we give what we can, it is sure to help us as well as other people."

They listened, and Mother Nature's advice was followed so well that every flower in the garden yielded her honey to the first Bee who wanted it, and every single seed grew into a strong healthy plant.

WHO KNOCKED?

A new family from the city had just moved into Pleasant Cottage. Pleasant Cottage was well named, for besides being a bright, sunny house with many rooms, as is the way with cottages nowadays, it stood in the midst of a large lawn where many trees grew luxuriantly. In the spring, when the branches were covered with all the shades of tender green, this was certainly a beautiful spot.

It was the second day after their arrival that they heard a knocking. Oh, dear me, how provoking it was! for though one may be glad to see one's friends and neighbors, it is just a little bit better if they do not call as soon as one has moved, but wait until there has been time to get things in place.

This is what the new family thought. But the knocking kept on so steadily that they were sure this neighbor meant to be heard. So Bridget left her work and went down to the door, grumbling all the way. "Well, if folks must be calling, why don't they ring the bell like decent people?"

But when she reached the front door and flung it open, not a person was there to see her cross look.

"It's the side door you're trying, then, is it?" said Bridget, hurrying around to that, and opening it with a still more spiteful fling and even a crosser look.

It certainly was strange, but that porch was just as empty as the front one had been. Then Bridget *was* cross, and muttered: "Well, if it's anybody calling on us in my kitchen they'll not be seeing us, for I won't let them in. But I'll have to look who's there, they keep on so."

So around to the kitchen she went, and when that opened door disclosed nobody, Bridget was indeed surprised. Upstairs she went, sure that some bad boy was fooling her by running from one door to another.

But, though she searched carefully, no mischievous lad came into sight, and still the knocking kept on. Then Bridget journeyed into the cellar and searched that. But again she found no one.

If there had been a house nearer, they might have thought that the noise was made by some workmen busily hammering. But the nearest dwelling was too far away for them to imagine that, so they concluded it must be a noise peculiar to the country.

And they were quite right, though it was not until late in the afternoon that they really did find out who knocked, and then the small boy of the family made the discovery, as small boys often do.

In great glee he shouted: "Mother, please come quick! I want to show you who knocked at the door this morning."

Mistress and maids, in fact the whole household, hurried down the stairs and out of doors, eager to solve the mystery.

In one corner of the lawn stood a tall, wide-spreading maple, and the small boy hurried them down the path, through the winding drive and across the soft green sod to that very tree. There, on a big limb, high above the ground, was a large brown and white speckled bird, with yellow wings and a bright red head. And as they watched they saw that the noise that had caused such confusion in their household all day had been wrought by this little creature, hammering against the wood with his sharp bill.

So surprised a family as they were then one does not often see.

All except the mother, who said: "Oh, it's a flicker or high-holder; how stupid I was not to think of it before! We used to have so many at our home in the country."

"It's a smart bird, anyhow," said Bridget, "to be fooling the whole of us."

After that, of course, the family were very much interested in the bird carpenter, and not a day passed that someone did not go to see how he was getting on. Day after day he hammered away with his sharp bill, digging the hole larger and deeper, until the ground all about was covered with tiny chips.

When the hole was about two inches deep, the work suddenly ceased, to the great disappointment of the small boy.

"Oh, mother, he's gone, and hasn't built a nest at all, as you told me he would," he complained.

"That's because Mr. Flicker, to use his other name, has found the wood is too hard. He can work only on wood that is beginning to decay, and after he had gone in that distance it was too hard for him to make any impression on it. At least, that is what I have always thought, though some of the bird books say that flickers have a fashion of building or boring several holes that they never expect to use. But he won't give it up entirely, so we will be on the watch to see and hear where he goes next time."

Accordingly the mother and the small boy listened and looked, and next day they heard, and soon after saw, the little carpenter busily drilling away at an apple-tree.

This, however, soon proved too much for him, and before the end of the week they heard his "wick-wick-wick" and saw him on a leafless bough of the old oak-tree near the dining-room windows. This evidently was just the place he wanted. Perhaps Madam High-holder had expressed a preference for a house finished in oak. At all events he drilled and bored day after day. And I am sure the only reason he did not sing or whistle at his work was because to do that is hardly possible when one uses his mouth for a tool; but he certainly worked very cheerily and faithfully.

If drawn with a compass the hole would not have been more truly round. It grew deeper and deeper, until one day Mr. High-holder thought it quite large enough. Then it was lined with hair and feathers to make it soft and warm for the six eggs Mrs. High-holder was to lay there and for the six young birds who were to live there after a while.

When it was all done, the gardener one day placed

a ladder against the tree, and the small boy and various members of the family clambered up softly one after another to take a look at the new home.

Even Bridget was there, and as she safely reached the ground she said: "You're the smartest bird I ever saw, fooling me all day with your knocking, and going to three trees one after another, till you found one that suited you for your nest!"

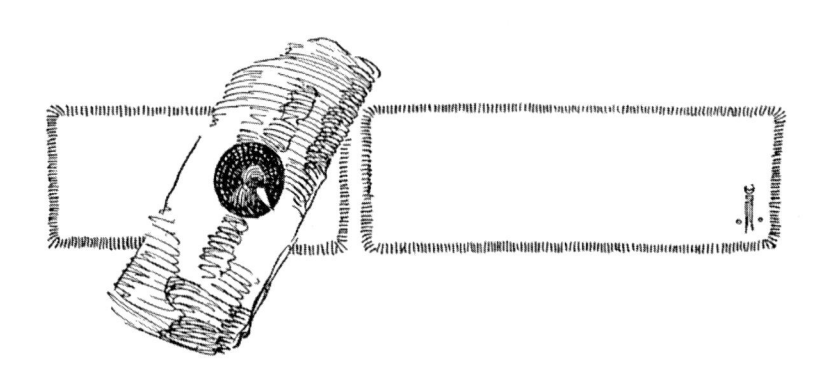

A DISOBEDIENT TREE

Once upon a time, a little boy was walking along in the soft grass, eating some cherries. That is not strange, is it? for there have been stories about little boys and cherries—ever since there have been little boys and cherry-trees, I had almost said; certainly, ever since there have been stories.

But in almost all of the stories of boys and cherries that I have ever read, the boys have been disobedient, and the cherries stolen or green, and after eating them the little boys have become very ill and have missed all sorts of good times.

So my story will be a little different, for the cherries were not stolen, but the little boy had gathered them off a tree at his own home. And they were not green, but just big, and ripe, and red—the very sort of cherry you and I would eat now if we had the chance.

And so, though he ate many more of them than he counted, he was not ill, but next day he was quite ready to eat more. He did not even swallow the pits, but dropped them on the ground as he walked.

One fell into a soft place and lay there a little while until the rain fell. As more rain came and the ground grew softer, this particular stone sank down, down, quite out of sight. It lay very quiet, there, until the hard outside of the pit grew soft and probably split apart.

Now, though we never should have thought so from looking at the outside, there was hidden away within this hard cherry-stone a germ of life. If I should write many pages, I could never make you understand, for I do not understand myself, how the sun, and the rain, and the air, and the earth, fed and helped and strengthened this speck till it burst through that hard outside and began to grow. It was very weak and hardly above the ground at first; then it showed two small green leaves, gaining a little every day, until, as the days and the weeks and the months went by, it was quite plain to everyone who looked that it was a cherry-tree.

It seemed to be a well-behaved tree, for as soon as it was old enough it bore blossoms which changed into cherries, after the fashion of cherry blossoms. It allowed the birds to build a nest in its branches. It let the bees get some of its honey. And though it had very few, it even gave up some of its best cherries to a family of robins who lived near.

But, like some girls and boys I have known—yes, and grown-up people too—this Cherry-Tree had one bad fault which kept it from being quite perfect. Every morning, as the sun rose in the east, it felt so nice and warm, that the Cherry-Tree sent its roots and rootlets toward the east and bent its head in that direction too. At first this was so very little that no one noticed it.

That is, no one but Mother Nature, who sees and understands all the faults of her great family of growing things.

A Disobedient Tree

So she said to the Cherry-Tree, in the language that plants alone understand, something like this: "My child, you must stand up straight, or the first thing you know you will be growing round-shouldered or hump-backed. And you must not send all your roots toward the east. That is such a bad habit that you Cherry-Trees have."

Then I fancy the little tree replied: "Oh, Mother Nature, I can't stand up straight. I like to have the sun kiss me good-morning. And it is easier to send my roots out toward the east. I think the ground feels warmer there."

"Nonsense!" said Mother Nature. "The sun could kiss you just as well if you held your head straight; and all the earth around you is warmed alike. It may be a little harder now for you to send roots in other directions, you have grown this way so long. But you must try this very day."

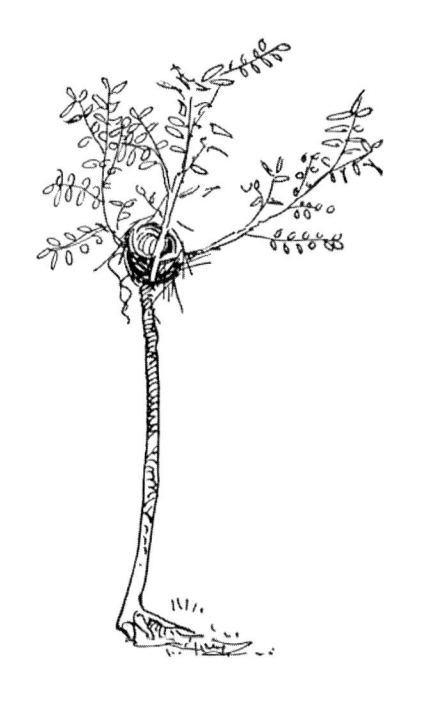

So, to be obedient, the Cherry-Tree really held its head straighter, and honestly tried to send roots out toward the west, the north, and the south. But it was harder, the ground did not seem so soft and mellow, so it soon gave up.

Like the teachers in our school, Cherry-Tree's teacher had been watching, and when she saw how soon it stopped and how short those roots were, she said: "To grow right you must grow in every direction. And you must not give up a lesson just because it is hard. What would become of the boys and girls in the schoolhouse over yonder if they did only the easy things? I am afraid their day would be all games and no lessons."

So the Cherry-Tree tried once more to grow in every direction, but as that still seemed hard, it soon gave up and had only short little roots on all sides but the east.

The years went on, and Mother Nature said no more to Cherry-Tree, because she knew it was too late, for it was now a full-grown tree. It was large and healthy looking and when it was covered with cherries it was really beautiful to see, except that down by the ground there were on the east side great rough roots, while the sod was quite smooth in every other direction.

One hot day in June a great black cloud came up in the west. The thunder muttered and growled and rumbled. All the air grew very still. Then a fluttering went through the trees, as though they were saying to one another: "Hold on tight, there's a big wind coming."

And suddenly, a big wind, almost like a tornado, did come. It struck the trees all around and twisted their branches so that some of them fell off, but the strong thick roots held the trees fast; that is, all but the Cherry-Tree. It had such very small roots on that side to hold with that the great wind soon tore them loose. And then, alas, the beautiful tree lay at full length on the ground.

When Mother Nature saw it she sighed as she said: "Oh, those Cherry-Trees! I wonder if I can ever teach them to grow in every direction and not just toward the east."

A Disobedient Tree

Probably the only way in which you and I can learn whether or not she succeeded is by noticing all the cherry-trees we meet.

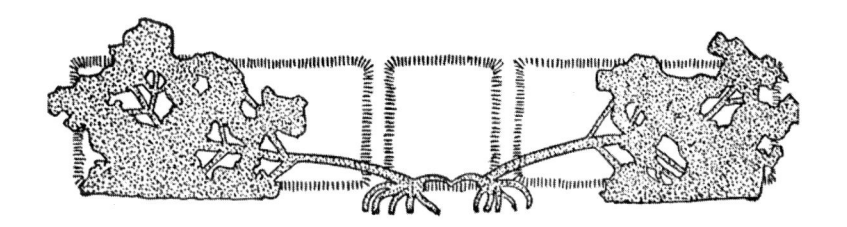

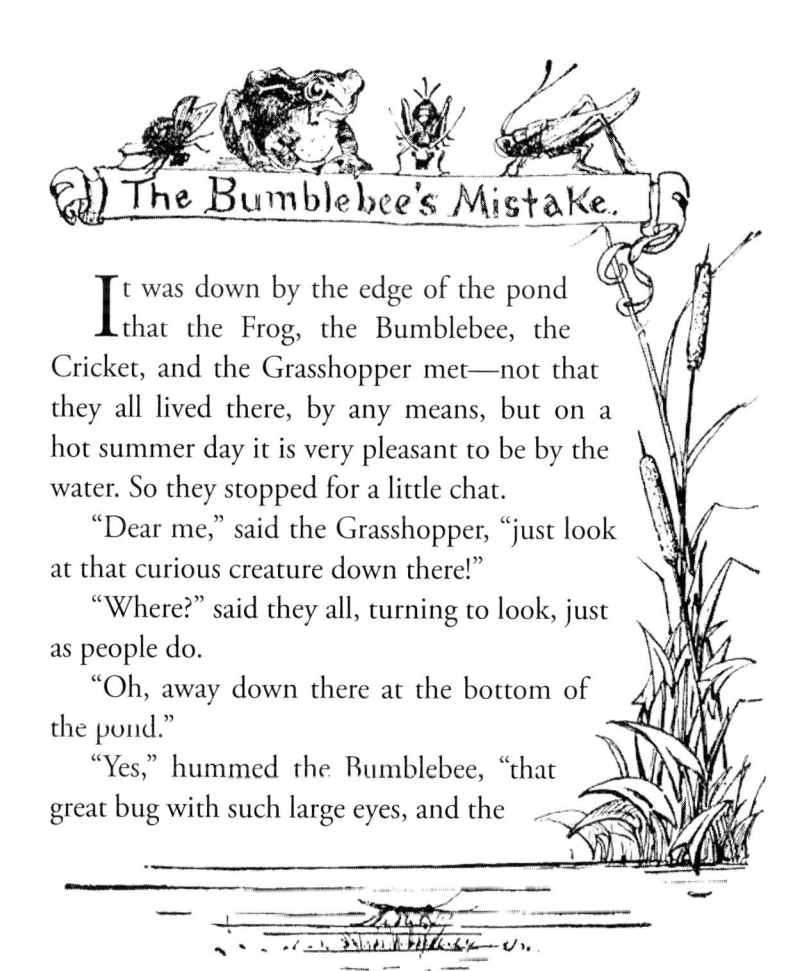

The Bumblebee's Mistake.

It was down by the edge of the pond that the Frog, the Bumblebee, the Cricket, and the Grasshopper met—not that they all lived there, by any means, but on a hot summer day it is very pleasant to be by the water. So they stopped for a little chat.

"Dear me," said the Grasshopper, "just look at that curious creature down there!"

"Where?" said they all, turning to look, just as people do.

"Oh, away down there at the bottom of the pond."

"Yes," hummed the Bumblebee, "that great bug with such large eyes, and the six long legs. He must be a stranger here; at least I have never seen him before."

"See how fast he walks along under the water," chirped

the Cricket; "he seems to be gobbling up something."

"Yes, he does act as though he were hungry," laughed the Grasshopper. "Perhaps Mr. Frog can tell us something about him, as he must be one of his neighbors."

"He has not been here very long," explained the Frog in answer to this. "A long while ago, in my tadpole days, a lovely creature came one day and dropped some eggs there on that large leaf under the water. After the hot summer days came, the eggs disappeared one morning, and I saw this queer bug there instead. He has some brothers and sisters down there, too, and they keep very busy flying about."

"Well, he may be busy, but he certainly isn't handsome," said the Bumblebee, thinking of his own coat of black and gold.

"Indeed he is not," answered they all, each one sure that he was very much handsomer than the Frog's ugly neighbor down in the pond.

One day not long afterward, the Bumblebee flew that way again. Perhaps it was so warm that he wanted to cool off, or it may be he thought that he would like a word with the Frog.

After he had been there some time, he looked into the water and asked: "Where is the ugly, long-legged bug I saw when I was here before?"

"Oh, it was funny about him," said the Frog. "He kept on growing and growing until he was actually too large for his skin."

"What happened then?" asked the Bumblebee.

"The skin split all the way down the back and out crawled that insect you see there."

The Bumblebee's Mistake

"That isn't the ugly bug, is it?"

"Yes, the very same."

"Well, he is not very beautiful to see yet, though rather better than he was before," murmured the Bumblebee, still thinking of his own good looks.

"He does a lot of work down there, any way, killing those tiresome mosquitoes," said the Frog.

But the Bumblebee flew away, for he did not care about hearing others praised. So he hurried to the meadow and amused the Cricket and the Grasshopper with a very funny account of how the long-legged bug with the large eyes had changed in his appearance. But he said never a word about the bug's good works, which seems rather mean.

So they all lived their lives, through weeks and weeks, going to the pond occasionally, where they often saw their former acquaintance down under the water eating mosquito eggs as fast as possible.

But one day when the Bumblebee went to call upon the Frog no one else was to be seen. So the Bee inquired: "Where is that queer neighbor of yours, the mosquito-catcher?"

"Well," croaked the Frog, "it is such a long story that

you would better sit here on the ground beside me while I tell it, or take this nice green rocking-chair here," hopping up beside a swaying grass.

So the Bee accepted the offered seat, and as he swung comfortably back and forth, the Frog said: "You remember that I told you how the bug outgrew its skin once before. Well, after it had changed it kept on growing and working. But one morning I missed it from its old place in the water and wondered where it could be. Very soon, though, I found it on the stem of that lily over there near the edge of the water. And, would you believe it? its skin began cracking again and split down the whole length of its back. Then out came something that looked like a large fly. For an hour or two it kept very quiet, then it unfolded its wings and flew away."

"Flew!" exclaimed the Bee, in surprise. "I never dreamed of its flying. How did it look?"

"Yes, flew, and faster than I ever saw any other insect fly too," croaked the Frog.

"It has a real long, slender body, like a cylinder."

"I like short, thick ones, better, myself," said the Bee.

"It had a great head with real large eyes, a short neck and four wings—but, there, you can see for yourself," finished the Frog.

And as the Bee looked up he saw coming toward him the very loveliest creature in all the insect world.

"You don't mean that this was ever that ugly bug?"

"The very same." Then, as it came nearer, "Let me introduce him to you—this is Mr. Dragonfly, Mr. Bumblebee."

"I have seen Mr. Bee before, I think, and heard some

of his remarks, though I have never had the pleasure of speaking to him."

The Bee looked at the beautiful Fly with its lovely colors. He saw the ten rings around its body, its six legs, its two feelers, and the pretty gauze wings, and really knew not what to say. Then he buzzed out: "Well, really, you have changed so much that I did not recognize you. I had no idea that you would ever be a darning-needle." There the Bee stopped, for he did not know how the Dragon-Fly would like that nickname.

"I know the children call me that, but it is only because they don't know me very well."

"I'm sorry," said the Bee.

"Well, I don't mind, for I do my best, and never hurt them—not even by stinging. Now suppose we have a flying match."

But there poor Bumblebee soon found himself beaten, for the Dragon-Fly was soon out of sight. Presently he came circling back.

"Did I go too fast for you?" Then, without even waiting for an answer, he continued: "Can you fly backward?"

The poor Bumblebee was filled with confusion as the Dragon-Fly flew backward and forward, to the right side or to the left.

"Isn't that wonderful! Is that all you can do?"

"Oh, no, I am working most of the time, trying to rid people of mosquitoes and flies, like this see!"

And as the Bumblebee looked, the Dragon-Fly, flying all the time, caught up a mosquito with its feet and put it into its mouth.

The Bumblebee was silent with surprise, but he learned

then and there never to laugh at people until he knew what they could do.

A BRAVE PLANT

It was a beautiful garden. Along one side grew the flowers,—lovely roses, smiling pansies, bright-eyed phlox, fragrant mignonette, and spicy pinks. But the rest of it was given up to things useful instead of beautiful, and there long straight rows of vegetables were to be seen.

There were graceful bean vines climbing as fast as possible to the tops of their tall poles, substantial cabbage heads, rows of cauliflower, mingled with the tender green of lettuce, luscious peas, crisp radishes, and every other vegetable to be found in a well-regulated garden.

As visitors walked around and through the well-kept paths, the vegetables vied with the flowers in claiming admiration.

In a corner of this beautiful garden lived still another class of plants, and if, attracted by spicy odors, you had gone that way, you would have found fragrant lavender, thyme, sage, wormwood, summer savory, and the old-fashioned herbs that used to have a place in your great-grandmother's garden, but which many little people like you have never seen.

A Brave Plant

Among these plants was one with grayish-green leaves, which had evidently come there to live only a little while before. Just as it had begun to take root and to send its leaves up through the ground, the gardener sent his helper there to pull the weeds.

He was not so careful as the gardener, and in moving around placed his great heel right on top of the plant.

Fancy how you or I should feel if some horrible monster, a thousand times as large as we, should step on our heads and crush us to the earth. So this poor little plant shivered through all its leaves and roots and thought it must surely die.

But Mother Nature whispered to it: "Try again, you are stronger than you think."

And to make it easier, the gardener, scolding all the time about his helper, loosened the earth, and tried to straighten the broken leaves.

So, helped and strengthened, the little plant did try again. It put forth more leaves in place of the bruised and broken ones. And as it began to feel stronger, it pushed another little stalk up through the earth.

The gardener smiled as he saw it, and, calling his careless helper, said: "See there, Mike, the Chamomile is going to live after all, though you did all you could to kill it."

It would have gotten on all right then but for that golf ball. The boys were striking balls about on the lawn one day, instead of waiting until they got to the links. And, alas, one of the balls flew over the garden fence and straight into the particular spot where the Chamomile grew. The ball might not have hurt so much, but the boy soon followed the ball and jumped down right into the middle of the plant.

Again the leaves were all bruised and bleeding. And again the poor plant felt that it never could live in so hard a world.

But again, too, Mother Nature whispered to it: "Be brave, you must not give up now. You have something to live for. Get strong as fast as you can, for there are people out there in the world whom you must help."

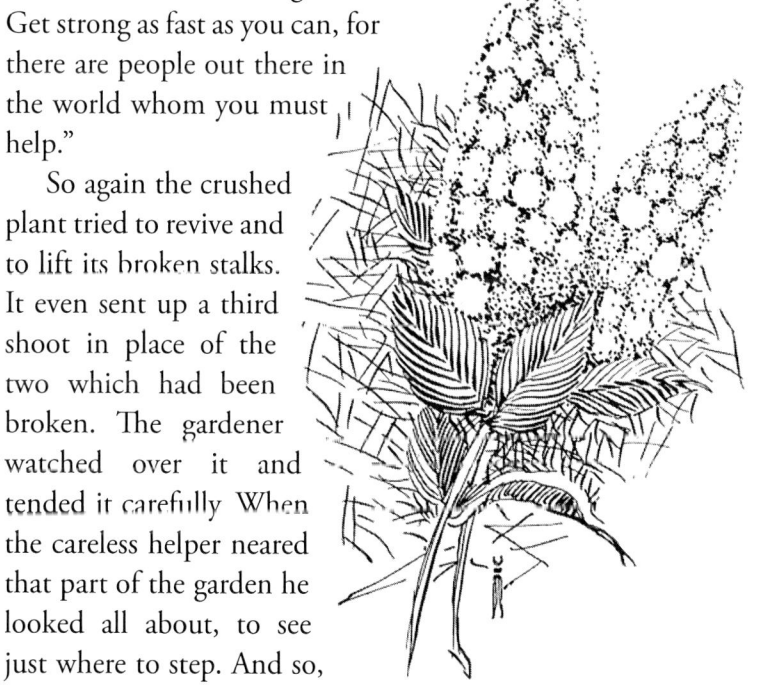

So again the crushed plant tried to revive and to lift its broken stalks. It even sent up a third shoot in place of the two which had been broken. The gardener watched over it and tended it carefully. When the careless helper neared that part of the garden he looked all about, to see just where to step. And so, as the days went by, the unfortunate Chamomile began to be a strong, healthy-looking plant.

But its misfortunes were not yet over, though it seemed to have had its share.

One Sunday morning when the gardener and Mike were neither of them to be seen, and consequently there was no fear of being driven out, Fido, the great Newfoundland puppy, thought it a good time for him to view the garden.

So, easily jumping the low fence, he was soon inside. At first he walked soberly up and down the paths, as properly as you or I might have done—not gathering or even stooping down to smell any of the beautiful sweet flowers which grew there.

But at last he spied a sunny corner which he thought would be just the place for a nap, as the morning was a trifle cool. Probably no one would have objected to that, for sometimes the very best thing for mischievous puppies, as well as for mischievous children, to do, is to lie down to take a nap.

The unfortunate thing about this, however, was that the very corner the dog chose for his bed was the particular spot where the Chamomile grew. And when he threw his large body down on the plant the stalks which had tried so hard to grow were again broken to the earth. No wonder that now the plant thought that all that was left for it was to die. It surely was not worth while to try to live in a place where it was always being hurt.

But again it heard the whisper which all the outdoor world must obey: "It is hard, I am sorry, but you must bear up. You cannot die now. Your flowers are to bring health to those who are ill. Some doctor may need them for medicine. Never mind your troubles; hold up your head and do your best."

So, because of this, the Chamomile tried once more. And in spite of its many mishaps, it began growing again, even sending out a root in another place and new branches up through the earth.

This time is was not so unfortunate. It grew steadily, with no heavy foot or wallowing dog to disturb it. Soon flower buds began to form and before long there were many spikes of the bitter white flowers.

As the gardener gathered a large bunch of them he said: "Well, that is well done for a plant with as hard luck as this has had! But that is always the way with this Chamomile; the more it's crushed, the more it spreads."

THE SOWER

"Wake up! wake up!" roared the March Wind.

The Pussy willows that had been lying asleep all winter stirred uneasily.

"Oh, it is so cold, I can't!" said one after another.

"Cold?" said the March Wind. "Don't you know there has been a new leaf turned on the calendar? The sun shines bright, and spring is here."

"Oh, but you sound so cold!" said one Pussy Willow.

"True, I may sound a little fierce, but I can't help it. It is my nature to. And with such warm fur overcoats to wear as you have I don't think you need to complain of the cold."

"Just let us sleep a little longer," pleaded the Pussy Willows. "Perhaps our fur coats are not done."

"Yes, they are all finished, and some of your family are out. Mother Nature had them done on time, though this is a very busy season with her."

"Has any one else come?" asked the Pussy Willows. It was so much easier to talk when warmly covered up than to stick one's head out into the cold.

"Oh, yes," answered the March Wind; "but I have not

the time to tell you about them. Come out and see for yourselves. I want to coax all the Catkins out to-day. I must melt the last snow-drifts away. I must blow the ice out of the river. Oh, I have so many things to do!"

So the March Wind rushed on.

The Pussy Willows said to one another: "Now we are so wide awake, perhaps we might just as well get up."

So they stretched themselves and put their heads out of their winter covering, and they were no sooner out than each one was dressed in his gray fur coat.

"Isn't this nice?" said one.

"Yes, and not the least bit cold," said the others.

"Oh, look! there is a woodpecker over on that apple-tree, getting spiders' eggs from under the bark for his dinner."

"Yes, he doesn't seem to see us, and see!—there is a robin."

"To be sure! I am glad the robins are back. And just hear that 'caw, caw.' "

"Yes, I should know Mrs. Crow's voice anywhere."

"And do see the crocuses! I am glad we came, aren't you?" asked Pussy number two, full of the spring-time gladness.

"Indeed I am. March Wind is really not half so bad as he sounds."

As the days went by and all the Catkin folk came out, the Pussy Willows were still more glad. There were the Beeches, the Alders, and the Willows, each covered with the graceful hanging Catkins. They grew in the warm sunshine, listened to the birds singing of their plans for another summer, saw the buds swelling on the other trees, and were sure, in plant-fashion, that it was a very good sort of world to be in.

"I want to stay here just as long as I can, don't you?" said one Catkin to another.

"Yes, but none of us ever remain very long; perhaps, though, if we hang on with all our might we need never fall."

"You need not talk that way," said one, wiser than the rest. "March Wind will blow so hard some day that you will let go just from fright, and drop on the ground as Catkins always have done."

"You'll see that we shan't," said they in chorus.

"Oh, no they won't!" echoed the Pussy Willows.

And they really all meant what they said. But one day March Wind came blustering and howling back. He was really making more noise than on the day when he wakened the Pussy Willows and tore such a great hole in their bedclothes that they had to get up and put on their fur coats.

"Oh, dear! what do you want?" said an Alder Catkin.

"What are you making such a noise about?" said the Beech.

"I am sorry you are not glad to see me, but that is always my fate. I have never yet known any one who loved a March wind. I really began well this year, and at first I was as gentle and lamb-like as could be. So you might forgive me if I roar like a lion to-day. March is going out to-night."

"Good-bye, then," said the Catkins great and small, Willow and Alder and Beech, trying to be polite, since for a whole year March Wind would be heard no more.

"Not quite so fast, my Catkin friends," blustered March Wind. "I have one more thing to do for you before I go."

"For us?" asked the Alder Catkin.

"Yes, for as many of you as I can," roared March Wind so that none could fail to hear.

"Thank you so much; you were very kind to our family once, but we really do not need any more help now," said the Willow.

"Oh, yes, you do," answered the March Wind. "The Pussy Willows thought they needed no help, but afterward they were glad I called them."

"What is it you mean to do for us?" asked the Beech Catkin, who, more wise than the others, wanted to know what the help was before refusing it.

The Sower

"I just came this way to help off as many of you as I could," said the March Wind, more gently, as though he were saving his breath for a very strong gust by and by.

"To help us off?" said the Willow.

"We don't want to be helped off," shivered the Beech.

"We just agreed that we would hang on all summer, and until real cold weather comes," said the Alder.

"That would be too late for you to do your work, Catkin folks. Don't you know I am the sower for you, and you must let me help you off and scatter you all around so that there may be more Willows, and more Alders, and more Beeches in the years to come?"

Then the Catkins understood, and when the March Wind roared like a real lion, and blew his hardest, they loosened their stems, and let him blow them all where he would, so that they might be trees by and by.

The Baby Plants' Bed Coverings

It was a baby Fern last May, but it grew bravely on week after week, weaving its lovely gown of green, until it was quite grown up. Then it plainly tired of all green, for it began weaving brown spots on the back of each leaf. If you or I had asked questions about these same brown spots, some one would have told us that they were to make new ferns another year. And if you had watched you might have seen, some day in the late summer, each of these seed pods break and scatter a brown powder around.

Then probably you would have asked another question and would have been told that the brown powder was pollen. And after that you would have asked no more, because you know that pollen is the powder which makes the seed babies grow another year.

So now the work of the large ferns was done, but how were the tiny ones to live all winter in the cold and ice?

Mother Nature is a wise old dame, and makes provision for many things. So she had thought of that, and early last May she had begun making her patchwork quilts.

If you had been a little girl in your grandmother's time, you would have known that it takes many stitches and much time to make a quilt. And Mother Nature was anxious that her quilts should be all ready for her seed babies before the cold weather came.

The blocks were green, but of every shape and size, and they looked very pretty as they hung on the trees to dry. You may think it strange, but each tree had a kind of its own. On the maples they were shaped something like a hand with five points, like five out-stretched fingers. On the oak they were longer, and scalloped along the edge. The lindens' were nearly round, with a point at one end, and every tree was unlike its neighbor. Some day gather all the leaves you can, and try to tell just what kind of tree each one came from. Then you will understand better how many patterns Mother Nature must have for her quilts.

All through the long summer days and nights the quilt blocks hung there. Then when October came, Jack Frost came too, and painted all the leaves. In a wonderfully short time they were all sorts of beautiful reds and yellows.

The trees looked very lovely then. But the blocks for

the quilts never seem to hang long after they are painted. And so, not many days after that, North Wind came along and pulled them all off the trees and dropped them on the ground.

But Mother Nature knew just which of the seed babies needed the most warmth, so she wanted more coverings in some places than others. She is so well supplied with helpers that she always has some one to do her bidding. So this time she called for her servant, East Wind, and he rolled and tumbled the leaves into piles, just where they were needed the most.

One less wise than Mother Nature would know that these leafy quilts would not stay that way long. Of course she knew it, and said: "Now I must have the rain to keep them in place."

So the rain came, and fell for a whole day on the leafy bed-quilt, until it lay quite flat over the baby ferns beneath. By this time, however, the blocks had lost their beautiful colors and were a dreary brown.

"Oh, dear me!" said the careful mother; "the nights are getting so cold now, I am afraid this is not near thick enough for them. Besides, there is nothing so nice for quilts as white. That is what I will try to get for a spread."

Before the week was out she had called upon her servant North Wind for a heavy snow-white blanket.

"With pleasure," said the North Wind. "But, dear Mother Nature, I have nothing to make it of. If you will get me some material you shall have a fine thick blanket."

"Oh, there will be no trouble about that," answered Mother Nature.

So she hurried away to Old Ocean, saying: "Please, I

should like something for a blanket of snow."

Old Ocean sighed and moaned as he always does and answered: "You are very welcome for stuff for your blanket if you can get it away. But you know I never deliver goods."

That did not trouble Mother Nature a bit. Since she has the whole world at her service, it is quite easy to have done whatever she wants. "There is old Father Sun, who has helped me before," she said; "I am sure he will be ready to oblige me now."

And she was not mistaken; for when the Sun heard her wants he sent some of his strongest Sunbeams to her aid. They kissed and coaxed the drops of water until the drops changed to vapor and went up, up, up, into the sky. After a while the sunbeams had drawn up so many drops of water that there were enough to make a cloud, and that was so heavy that Mother Nature knew she could soon have her

The Baby Plants' Bed Coverings

beautiful blanket. So she called damp, chilly East Wind to help her. And they squeezed and pressed that rain cloud so hard that the vapor from Old Ocean became drops of water again, ready to fall on the ground.

"I want a blanket for my baby plants, instead of rain," said Mother Nature. "So, Jack Frost, you must come to my aid this time."

So before the raindrops had gone very far from the cloud, Jack Frost touched them with his icy fingers. And straightway there was such a change that you would have thought the fairies had been at work. Every raindrop was changed into a beautiful snow crystal. There were as many shapes as there had been among the leaves that had fallen from the trees. Mother Nature was much pleased. The crystals fell all day and all night, and when the morning came, not a single tiny plant was to be seen, because they were all so well covered with a thick blanket of snow.

And when the spring came again, the Fern babies and all the other plants were ready to lift their heads, just because Mother Nature's bed coverings had kept them so warm all winter.

A FAMILY QUARREL

It was a very busy time of year. The carpenters were building new houses, and the birds were making new nests as fast as they could.

So it was no wonder that Madam Wasp said to herself one day: "Really, I think it is quite time I began work on a new home. It is so pleasant that I will start out this very day and begin to get material. It is no small undertaking, since I have to make the paper as well as the house."

So Madam Wasp unfolded her wings and flew away to see about her new home. She was her own architect, so she had no need to wait for plans.

She hurried to the nearest ash tree and began tearing off bits of bark and wood. On the ground below her was a Caterpillar, watching her. But keeping quiet is rather tiresome; so soon the Caterpillar said: "Good morning, Madam Wasp; please excuse me for asking, but what are you doing?"

"Certainly," said Madam Wasp; "I am getting wood for my new house."

"Indeed? I never knew that Wasps occupied wooden

houses. In some way I had gotten the impression that their homes were built of paper."

"So they are; if you will watch I can soon show you."

Then, putting some of the wood into her mouth, the Wasp soon made it into a soft pulp. Then she patted it with her feet until it was a thin sheet, and the Caterpillar saw it dry into paper. When this was finished the Caterpillar bade her good-bye until another day and crawled away to his mate.

"Well, my dear," said he, "I met Madam Wasp to-day, and was very much interested in seeing her build her new house."

"That is strange," said Mrs. Caterpillar, "for I spent a very pleasant hour or two with Madam Wasp myself, this morning, and didn't see you."

"How remarkable! but it must have been another member of the Wasp family. Where did you meet her?"

"Down by the ash-tree in the meadow."

"How singular! for I saw her by the ash-tree, too. You must have left before I arrived. Isn't it curious to see her break off the pieces of wood?"

"Break off pieces of wood? You must mean dig up the earth."

"My dear Mrs. Caterpillar, you must be losing your faculties. Didn't I, myself, see Madam Wasp tear off the bits of wood, and didn't she explain to me how she made the wood into paper?"

"I don't see how you can talk so, Mr. Caterpillar. I, myself, saw her dig up the earth with her forefeet. She kept working so hard that I asked her what she was doing, and she told me she was making a home for herself."

"There is no use talking to you," said Mr. Caterpillar. "I shall just wait until to-morrow and then I will go again to see Madam Wasp, so that I can prove to you that she builds her house of paper."

"And I will go to see Madam Wasp, too, and ask her if she doesn't live in a hole, though I am just as sure as can be that she knows no more about making paper than I do."

And then the Caterpillars curled themselves up into balls, each too cross with the other to speak. When morning had come Mr. Caterpillar hurried off very early, so that before she was able to get away Mrs. Caterpillar saw him coming home.

As soon as he caught sight of her he began; "There, my dear, I hope you are satisfied now that I knew what I was talking about! I went to see Madam Wasp, and she told me she had never lived in the ground. That wood she made into paper yesterday is a stiff, hard sheet now. She makes a house and puts ever so many layers of paper around it, and—"

But Mrs. Caterpillar interrupted him with, "I am going to see Madam Wasp this minute, though I know her house is in the ground."

So away she crawled, and before very long was back with the words: "There, I knew I was right! Madam Wasp was busy clearing away the pile of dirt she dug out yesterday. It was so high that it was in her way, so she got on it with her feet, and threw the dirt back of her with all her might. And she lives in a hole in the ground, instead of in a paper house, as you tried to make me think."

"My dear, I am sorry you are so positive," said Mr. Caterpillar, much vexed because the other was so self-willed. "I know very well what I am talking about; but, since you will not believe me, come with me and see for yourself."

"You will go with me, and see for yourself, you mean," answered Mrs. Caterpillar.

And they both crawled away.

"Is this the way you go?" asked Mrs. Caterpillar.

"Yes; I think it is the nearest."

She said no more until they reached the meadow.

When they had nearly crossed it she exclaimed in surprise: "Is that the ash-tree you meant?"

"Yes; isn't it the one you were talking of?"

"Oh, no; mine is down there farther."

"So we didn't mean the same Wasp either?"

"No; I am sorry."

"Well, since we are here, I want you to see the paper house."

Mrs. Wasp showed them how she made the wood into paste, and the paste into paper. Then she explained that her house was going to be oval with many layers of paper for the outer walls, and with a door in the bottom. Inside there would be ever so many little cells, each one made of paper. These little cells were to be on different floors, and the floors to be fastened together with little rods. The cells in the five upper stories were smaller, for there the workers lived. And down below were three floors of larger rooms, for several families of Wasps were to live in this house.

"There!—what did I tell you?" said Mr. Caterpillar, in triumph.

"Yes, I see that you are right; but come with me, and you will see I was, too," said Mrs. Caterpillar.

So they crawled to the other ash-tree, and the other Wasp, and then Mr. Caterpillar saw that this Wasp did live in a hole in the ground which she had dug with her feet. Her house did not need to be so large as that of the social wasp; only one family was to live in this one.

They both learned, too, that this wasp was fond of Caterpillars. She was hungry and thought one of them would make a nice dinner. But just as she was about to sting Mrs. Caterpillar in the head, so that she might carry her into her hole, Mr. Caterpillar saw and gave warning.

"Dear me, what a narrow escape you had!" said Mr. Caterpillar, as they hurried away.

"Yes. And what a foolish quarrel we had. I never will contradict you again."

"Nor I you, for we might both be right, just as we were this time."

TWO TRUE STORIES ABOUT ROBINS

The first of these stories is about a robin which is now living in Philadelphia.

About eight years ago, when he was a baby robin, he hopped out of the nest to try to fly. But his little wings were not so strong as he thought. So, though he succeeded in getting out of the nest to the ground, try as hard as he could, he was not able to fly back again. When he had stretched his wings many times, as the mother robin had bidden him, only to flutter a little way and fall back, he gave up and hopped about on the lawn.

A kind lady was watching him from the window, and was so sorry for the poor little robin that she put him up on one of the lower branches of the tree. Even then, however, he was not strong enough to get back into the nest.

Now Philadelphia cats, like most other cats, are very fond of birds. So, to save the robin's life, the lady put him into a cage in the house, there to live until he should be grown.

When he had become a strong, large bird she opened the door of the cage, and the windows of the room, so that there might be nothing to hinder the robin from flying away to live with his friends out of doors. But he seemed to prefer his home in the cage to one in the trees, for he flew as far as the window sill, looked about him, and then went back to his cage. And there he has lived ever since. Often the chance of joining his relatives has been offered him, but he never accepts it, though he joins in their happy songs.

When the first warm days come in the spring his mistress hangs him in the open window, where he sings away as joyously as can be. Sometimes people who are passing will say: "Oh, there is a robin, the first one I have heard this spring."

And then they will walk very slowly, and look up among the branches of the trees to find the first robin of the season. But the robin and his mistress smile to see that the people cannot find him.

Last year a strange thing happened to this bird.

In July he lost his feathers, as robins do, but when the new ones came in, he found himself, instead of being dressed in brown with a red waistcoat as he had been all his life, all black. It was not shining, changing black feathers, like those the grackle blackbird wears, but dull, lusterless ones.

The robin never told us how he liked this change of

dress; but he evidently did not mind much, for he sang just as cheerily as ever. His mistress seemed to care more than he did. She was very glad when the next moulting time came, for then he lost his black feathers and put on brown ones with red for his breast, like those he had worn since his babyhood.

We have wondered often if out-of-door robins ever change their color; or if in some strange way this caged bird heard of the death of his grandfather or grandmother and wore mourning for a little while.

The other story is of a Chicago robin and his nest.

Two or three years ago, late in July, a little brother and sister were playing under a tree on the lawn.

The boy happened to look up into the tree, when he exclaimed: "Oh, Grace, I see something red up there! I wonder what it is."

But though the little girl looked and looked, she had to say: "Where? I can't see anything but leaves."

"Right there on this side of the tree," answered her brother, pointing up into the leafy branches.

"Oh, yes; I see! That's a bird's nest with something bright in it," said Grace.

"I am going to climb up after it," exclaimed Edward.

"No, you must not. For see—the bird is on the nest."

They had both been taught not to disturb the birds. So as soon as Edward saw that Mrs. Robin was at home, he was quite willing to leave the nest alone. But the children told the other members of the family. One after another they stood under the tree, trying to find out what could be in the bird's nest.

At last, the robin mother was through sitting on her blue eggs, and had some tiny birds to feed. And after a while, the young birds grew to look as if they had bodies as well as mouths, and got their skinny selves well covered with feathers, and in due time flew away. When the nest was quite deserted, so that there need be no fear of frightening the young birds, Edward climbed into the tree. And what do you suppose he found woven into the nest for a lining?

It did not take him long to get back to the ground, exclaiming: "Would you believe it! The robins have a flag out. And that red we have seen so long is part of it."

"Oh," said mother, "I suppose it is one of those little ones you had for Fourth of July. You children scattered a good many of them about."

"Of course," said the father. "Well, those robins are

good Americans. I am sure so patriotic a nest as that should be saved."

So he sent the gardener, with a saw, up into the tree. He soon returned, bringing a branch with the nest on it. The family all looked, and wondered over the way in which the robin had used the little flag. And it was thought so curious for a robin to hang out the red, white, and blue, that the patriotic nest was sent to a museum in Chicago, where to-day you probably could see and wonder at it.

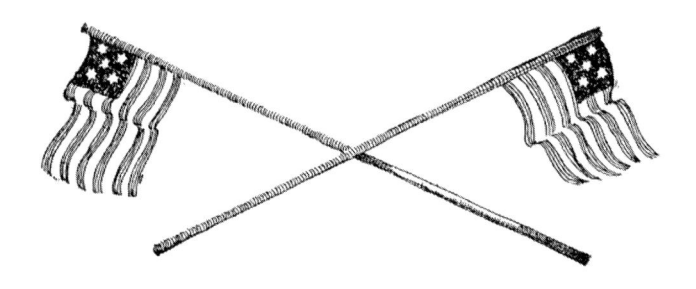

THE IDLE CHIPMUNK

It was a beautiful October day, just the kind of a day to have a good, happy time before one settled down to winter and hard work. So many of the outdoor people were about that day. They flew in and out among the falling leaves, or raced over them as they lay thick on the ground. But there was one little creature in reddish brown, with very bright black eyes and a bushy brown tail, that seemed too busy to stop for a moment.

Another chipmunk ran up to her, saying: "What makes you work so hard this lovely day? Come over to this fence rail and sit a while with me. I want to chatter with you." But the busy chipmunk answered: "Oh, no, I thank you; I haven't the time. I must get ready for winter."

"Get ready for winter—nonsense!" said the idle one. "Just feel this warm sun and then talk about winter! I am going to enjoy myself through some of this nice weather and after that I can work."

Then, looking up, she found she had no one to listen to her, for the busy chipmunk had hopped away out of sound if not out of sight, and was filling her pockets as fast as possible with acorns from the oak-tree. And such a curious place as her pocket was in! You know people sometimes laugh and say a woman's pocket can never be found, and make fun of all that a boy carries in his, but the chipmunk's was different from any you or I have ever seen. For there was one in each cheek.

When these strange pockets were full of nuts, she started off to her home. She ran along with her load until she came to her own house. You and I probably should not have found the front door, but Mrs. Chipmunk knew just where it was, which makes a great difference. She just whisked into a hole under the root of a tree and was in her own hall. This was not square like the halls people often build in their houses now, but was long and winding. But Mrs. Chipmunk had not the slightest trouble to find her store-room.

So she hurried into that and emptied her pockets, then started out for another load. And this she did day after day, until her store-room was filled with nuts.

Meanwhile, the idle chipmunk ran about and chattered with every one she met who would listen to her, until suddenly the bright sunny days were over, and there came a cold, frosty morning.

Then the busy chipmunk came out of her front door and looked about her. It was so unpleasant, however, that she did not stay long, but hurried back through her long, winding hall into her cosy sitting-room. She and her mate had taken much trouble to get this ready, too, and had carpeted it all with soft grass so that it should be nice and warm for their baby chipmunks.

"Really, my dear," said Mr. Chipmunk, "we are so nicely fixed here that I don't mind how soon winter comes."

"Nor I; for we have plenty of food in our store-room to last till spring."

Just then there was a noise at their front door. Then some one came down the long hall and into their warm room. And looking up they saw the idle chipmunk.

"Oh, dear, what shall I do?" she shivered. "We are so cold, and we have nothing in our house to eat, and winter has begun."

The busy chipmunk answered: "I told you the nice days wouldn't last always, but you would not listen to me."

"Yes, I know," chattered the idle one. "I am sorry; but couldn't you just give me a few loads of nuts out of your store-room to keep my family from starving to death?"

"No, indeed," said Mr. Chipmunk; "we shall need it all before summer comes."

But the busy Mrs. Chipmunk, mother like, thought of the baby chipmunks who must go cold and hungry, so she interrupted her mate by saying: "I am sorry we can't spare you anything, but we must think of our own family. But if you and Mr. Chipmunk would like us to, my mate and I will go out with you when the day gets a little warmer and help you gather something."

"It is more than I deserve," said the idle chipmunk; "but if you would be so kind I never could thank you enough."

So presently the busy chipmunks joined the idle one and her mate, who had set to work so soon as she had left them. All four worked with all their might, running back and forth with grass to line the nest and with nuts for the store-room. Oh, how busy they all were! The idle

The Idle Chipmunk

Mrs. Chipmunk thought many times of the hours she had spent chattering on the fence rails or the stone wall. If she had done something then, she need not have been so tired now.

Before many days they were all obliged to stop, for it grew too cold for chipmunks to be out. But the idle chipmunks' store-room was not empty now, though not nearly so full as that of their busy neighbors. Still, there was enough to keep them from starving and something to make their nest warm.

The days grew colder and colder, so both families of chipmunks curled themselves up to sleep. It was not just to sleep over night, but for days, until in the midst of the cold there came some mild weather. Then all the chipmunks awoke. The busy family brought out from their store-room many nuts and acorns. They all sat up and held the nuts in their forepaws, and ate and chattered and had a great feast.

But the other chipmunks could not eat much, because they had so little put away. They each had one nut, then the mother said: "Come, children, we must save the rest for another day. You would better go to sleep now, then you will forget how hungry you are."

Then as the idle chipmunk watched each hungry child lay his head on his tail for a pillow and cry himself to sleep, she said to her mate: "We never will be so lazy again."

And I am sure they never were.

The Troubled Apple Tree

It was the same Apple-Tree that we saw in the very first story. Many times it had lost its blossoms. Still, it did not feel so sorry for that now, for it knew it should find them again in the apples.

But it was very sad now, because all the trees that had stood beside it in the orchard were dead and gone, and no one seemed to care for the few blossoms that this tree could bear. And as for its apples, they lay on the ground unnoticed. No one wanted the knotty, wormy apples that grew on an old apple-tree.

So it was no wonder that Apple Tree's tears should fall thick and fast, or that she should think her best days were over and that it would be well for her to lie in the ground, dead like her companions.

But in the midst of her trouble came the voice of Mother Nature, saying, as it had said once before: "Wait a little longer, dear. Your time is coming, the time when you will be useful again."

Apple-Tree did not at all understand how this could be. She had never heard of an old apple-tree growing young again. Still, she believed what Mother Nature said was true, for the good dame always keeps her promises to her children. Apple-Tree's scanty crop of apples fell on the ground once more, and again every one passed them by.

Apple-Tree was so grieved to see it that she cried out: "Oh, Mother Nature, I am so tired! Must I wait very much longer?"

She felt almost young again when Mother Nature answered kindly: "No; help will come to you to-morrow."

So on the morrow Apple-Tree stood up bravely, for help was coming to her that day. But, though she looked hour after hour, nothing seemed to happen. She felt no younger nor stronger than she had the day before. Her leaves were just the same. In the afternoon a bird came and rubbed his beak over the rough bark, and that was all.

Apple-Tree was so disappointed that her tears fell, and she cried: "Oh, Mother Nature, you told me help should come to me to-day!"

"Yes, and it has come. Only you did not see it. Just trust me a little longer and you will see."

So the Apple-Tree waited as she had years before, and again, just as she had then, she learned that Mother Nature had told the truth. For one day, out from under the bark came a tiny shoot of yellowish green. Soon there were two small leaves, and then branches. Mother Nature had been right, after all, and the Apple-Tree had a new growth. Perhaps she would bear beautiful blossoms and fine large fruit again. How nice that would be!

But as the leaves and branches grew larger, instead of being dark, like the apple, they were a dull, yellowish green. And the Apple-Tree was much puzzled.

Still, she kept on giving her strength to the strange new plant that was growing from her branch. Daily it became stronger and larger, and put forth new buds. These buds grew into yellow flowers, though they were not so pretty as the pink and white ones which had once made her so lovely. But Apple-Tree knew they must be something worth having, for Mother Nature had promised her she should be useful again.

Once she ventured to ask: "Why did you tell me you had sent me help on that day so long ago? It was weeks afterward that there came that tiny bit of green."

Mother Nature answered, smiling: "Do you remember the bird who came that day and rubbed his beak over your bark?"

Yes, Apple-Tree remembered.

"Well, that bird had been eating mistletoe berries; some of the tiny seeds had stuck to his beak, and when he rubbed it against your bark the seeds caught there and grew."

"And all the time I was giving up hope," said the Apple-Tree.

"Yes, though I had promised you you should be useful again."

Now the sadness of the Apple-Tree was turned into joy. Passers-by no longer went on leaving it unnoticed. Instead, they came to gather branches from it. The mistletoe was carried into homes to bring merriment and gladness. And the Apple-Tree that bore it was honored more in its old age than in its youth, for any apple-tree can bear beautiful blossoms and fruit, but on very few grows the magic mistletoe.

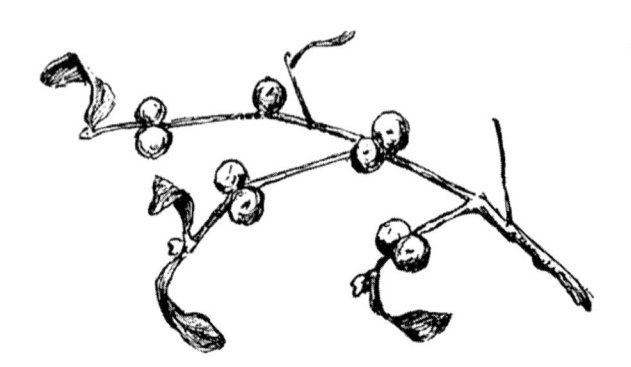

For more great resources
for your home school, visit
SimplyCharlotteMason.com